the ISLAND

a novelette

Eric Wiberg

illustrated by Yiwen Yan

Island Books

Copyright © 2024 Eric Tröels Wiberg & Yiwen Yan
ISBN 9781735632483 paper
Library of Congress Control Number: 2023942762

All rights reserved. No part of this publication may be reproduced in any manner without the prior written permission of the author, illustrator and publisher, except in the case of brief quotations embodied in articles or reviews. Contact eric@ericwiberg.com.

Layout and editing by Abdul Rehman Qureshi, writingpanacea@gmail.com

Published by Island Books, Boston, MA, USA

Printed in the United States of America

for Cait

Eric Wiberg text,
Yiwen Yan illustrations,
Abdul Rehman Qureshi layout,
Jacqueline Austin edits

also by Eric

Juvenilia: Teen Books & Travel Writing
Napoleon's Battles (with Felix Wiberg)
Yacht Voyages: One Captain's Adventures Afloat
Sea Stories
Travel Diaries
Scars: A Morbid Memoir
First Fifty in Fifty
Boston Harbor
Warplanes Lost & Found in The Bahamas
Round the World in the Wrong Season
Bahamas in World War II
Mailboats of the Bahamas
U-Boats in the Bahamas
U-Boats off Bermuda
U-Boats in New England
Drifting to the Duchess (script & book)
Åke Wiberg (with Mats Larsson)
Tanker Disasters (master's paper)
Published Writing (five editions)
Swan Sinks

Contents

I	1
II	4
III	6
IV	8
V	10
VI	14
VII	18
VIII	20
IX	24
X	29
XI	32
XII	34
XIII	36
XIV	38
XV	42
XVI	45
XVII	48
XVIII	50

I

There was a little boy who grew into a young man, then chose to live on a little island and go back to being a little boy. Even though his fingers sometimes hurt from touching things he discovered, he still yearned to touch more, to learn more.

He could not leave his little island, but the world came to him in the form of myriad objects. Though his physical needs were met, these things fed the hungriest of his organs: his mind, which required the greatest variety of stimulation.

If the boy could not leave, then what would arrive in his little world by sea or air? And how, if ever, would he regain the world of other people, and share his own world?

To understand the ending, we must start at a beginning.

This boy, like many of us, was born between two places. He was born between two parents, each from different places. One parent came from one side of a vast ocean, and the other across it. Some called this ocean a pond, but really, it wasn't. It was often boiled into a place mountainous with impassable waves, yet hours later could be smooth as a freshly-pressed table cloth.

As if to compromise—for he learned that compromise was important—the boy and his brothers and sisters were raised on a little island between the shores of the big continents. At first it seemed that the island was in the middle, like the triangle at the center of a see-saw. Grandparents from both sides, speaking different languages, would come to visit.

The family even visited both continents. But few things, even oceans, are always perfectly balanced. And so it was that the boy and his family tilted more to the western continent, which was much closer to their island. It became more difficult and took longer to visit the eastern continent, even though whole summers might be enjoyed playing, working, traveling, and studying there.

Before his first decade arrived, half of the brothers and sisters went away to the western continent to live at school. There they explored, played sports, and sent happy reports home.

At first.

II

Then it was the boy's turn. He went away the week he became a teenager.

His little brother stayed behind with the same metal soldiers they had played with together, staying in the bunk bed they had shared, now half-empty. They had pets—dogs, chickens, snakes, turtles, a cat, even ducks before the dogs ate them, and the snakes ate the chicken eggs.

For three years the boy grew and was happy. He turned into a young man. When he was barely shaving, he went to a new school.

Then he understood why the letters from his older brother and sister were less frequent. Then he understood why the letters were less happy. Then he understood why he smelled things like smoke and alcohol on people. Then he understood the furtive looks and fretful conversations between his parents.

The boy was beginning to understand a difference between how things were supposed to turn out, and how they actually turned out. School may end in June, but some students would go home well before it ended. Graduations, which look lovely in brochures, are less so when loved ones aren't involved.

Then he understood the phone calls to special tutors, rehabilitation clinics, headmasters, relatives, guidance counsellors, and psychotherapists. He understood why when he called his brother to say Happy Birthday he wasn't there, but in a clinic. Why the other brother wasn't at his school, but moved to another, up north in the cold. Why his sister had to go home for a while.

III

One day, while looking over the ocean from the new (but older) school, the boy made up his mind to run away. He had found a big, dead turtle on the beach and learned it had swum from the orient to the western continent, which was a long way to swim, even with four flippers. It had been tangled up in fishing nets and drowned, washing up at the school. Scientists took away its head for study.

The boy loved turtles, had always loved turtles. He loved that they could walk on land and swim in the sea and in ponds like he could. He loved that they could go from one country to another breathing the air and swimming the seas.

He loved that they were quiet, peaceful, and beautiful. Most of all, he loved and admired that the turtles had a strong shell to protect them from harmful creatures, and from other turtles. He learned that when turtles are young and need a hard shell the most, their shells are the softest; so that's when they need protectors the most.

Just before his shell was hard enough, it seemed that everyone got through the boy's soft shell, and all at once. The man taking care of his dormitory, and the man who was supposed to stop the man taking care of his dormitory, and the men and women above those two, and so on.

The dominoes fell all the way up to his own parents, who simply didn't believe that people did those kinds of things. So, just like the beatings when much younger, which formed the first cracks in his protective shell, these things didn't happen.

Except, they had.

Even with three missed graduations, the belief still held: the ending had to look like the brochure.

But the boy wanted to be like a turtle, wanted to quietly and beautifully slip out of his school into the water, and swim away and never look back.

IV

Sometimes there is a lag between when we decide to do a thing, and when we do it. In this case, the moment the boy went from deciding to run away to actually running away came during his first year of university, right after he escaped the second school.

This time he wasn't sitting on the shore looking at the sea. This time he was kneeling on the verge of a highway, with strangers, hearing that sound of zippers going up and down like the monorails at amusement parks.

This was so different from the brochures that it put the boy in a state of shock: an animal stunned in bright lights, having a hard time comprehending anything, making order of anything. Surviving long hitchhikes lasting days in freezing weather was so completely foreign to him and so jarringly different from his warm upbringing.

At first, he didn't swim away like a turtle. At first the boy, who was now a young man, swam away into a bottle. Mostly it was a gin bottle, but really any bottle would do.

And instead of rivers and oceans, he escaped any way he could: by foot, bicycle, bus, and plane.

V

    Gin and highways didn't allow the boy to get very far, though. And he always ended up back where he started. So, the boy found a new way to go away, and perhaps even reach the shores of the eastern continent; that new way was by sailing, for which one needed only wind. Unlike walking which was interrupted by deep water, sailing was enabled by it. You could go far without even fuel or a motor. On a sailboat, the water tank was more important than the fuel tank, you could catch food from the boat, and bring your bedroom and friends with you.

As a little boy, he learned the basics of how to sail on little boats inside the reef and on ponds and lakes. At the second school, he joined the sailing team but was quietly let go for absentmindedly wandering off alone like Ferdinand the Bull, daydreaming in the sun, smoking cigarettes and watching the breeze carry the gray tendrils through the rigging, and finding things on the sea surface far from the race course.

Watching them practice from the shores of a busy river, the boy saw that there were many sailboats tied up in the river in the middle of the big harbor city where he went to university.

One November night, the boy took one of those sailboats, which was less than 20 feet long, with barely a little cuddy up front—just one sail and boom, no motor, and wire rigging less than the diameter of a pencil.

That night the boy filled a pillowcase with cans of condensed soup, an opener, spoon, gallon jugs of water, a blanket, and a hand-held compass, and stowed them in the boat. Untying the little boat from the floating dock in the wide river, he pushed it into the water and pulled up the sails.

Then the boy headed down the river to where it met the harbor, thence it would take him to the ocean, and thence past a big cape shaped like a curled arm, and into the wide western ocean. Thence the winds (which rotated clockwise in that ocean) would carry him to the old continent, perhaps to exotic countries where they wore berets and ate long loaves of bread that could be used as oars.

The boy quietly sailed down the famous river, past universities, islands where the ducklings nested in spring, majestic granite bridges, and a gold dome and a museum to the sciences, until he reached a lock connecting the freshwater to salt: the river to sea.

He didn't have a radio. The lock's bridge was too low for the mast to go under. The lock was not operating for boats. There were no lights on. There was no way the boy could pull the mast down and up alone, or pull the boat over the concrete, or otherwise get through the lock.

The boy didn't know of any other boats to steal on the other side of the lock. There was a police station at the locks. It was dark and cold, and the place he found the boat was upwind from him, which is the hardest direction to sail.

Disconsolately, the boy turned around. One cannot steal a boat so easily in daylight that has a university's name printed on the hull and the sails, past a police station, and not expect to be caught.

Besides, he had classes the next day.

Dispirited but not broken, the boy tacked back and forth and sailed back to the floating dock. He tied the boat up, lowered and stowed the sails, and took his pillowcase over to the metro station, on the metro, and back up the heartbreakingly-long sloping hill lined with chestnut trees where he went to university.

He decided that to reach the other continent from his continent, he would have to find a bigger, safer boat (with a captain on it) who would take him on board, feed, and perhaps even pay him. The place to find such boats was in the seaports where he schooled or the islands where he had grown up.

So that is where the boy went.

VI

After his second year, the boy was accepted to an even older university in the eastern continent, on an island in fact, and so he set about sailing there. He sold his school books after his last exam, flew to a warm island, joined a sailboat with a young gregarious owner, and sailed from island to island, eventually to the old continent. The last leg of the voyage took three weeks. The crew and the boy weren't fed properly, and even the water was salty. They didn't have anything to drink, smoke, or snort. They fought with knives. At the time, the boy focused on the ship's cat, and on survival.

Once he got to the lovely cozy university and put on a blue and white linen bathrobe to ward off the November chill and warmed up with toddies of rum and whisky, smoking and writing alone by candlelight in a building built before the western country was a country, he wrote about the voyage.

Writing about things was a way for the boy to make sense of them, to frame them, to share them, and in a way to de-fang them. That night the boy began to write two pages for the college magazine about his voyage from one continent to another with crew from all over.

The sun rose the next morning to show the boy curled up at the base of the little standing sink, dark streaks under his eyes from crying for hours, shaking and trembling. He had written nineteen pages about the voyage, in a trance of sorts.

All those things he had put into the can—the fears and emotions; the anxieties about vulnerability; the recollection of two knife attacks, of missing two large islands through navigational error, of deafening roars from 40-foot seas and 67-knot winds followed by eerie silences and a wobbly steering wheel while the lone helmsman in his teens or twenties waited to be hurtled down waves at 15 miles per hour with no motor or sails set—all came back. They left him a jellied, helpless wreck.

Later, a man in a fancy bow tie and beard at another university would tell the boy that what he went through was reliving a trauma vividly. It was a way of processing scary events and some scientists call it PTSD, even if it wasn't from a war.

The problem with reliving the scary things for the boy was that, like a bit of string on a ball, it dangles other scary things—the ones that caused the traumatic stuff in the present nightmare—causing them to resurface as well. So, fear raises the question: why were you at sea in the first place?

And that goes back to the sordid stuff like zippers going up and down on the sides of highways. And that goes back to the sordid stuff in the windows overlooking the pretty quad at the pretty school. And that goes back to the teachers from an old island who beat the children in their care.

And that goes back to images found in shoeboxes in hotel attics and to nannies from other old continental countries, and back, and back, and back, until you become just a bug pinned to an examination table awaiting dissection, so little of you left, so spare your emotions that you feel you're a plucked hen and wish they would just pluck you like a guitar string - taut between two pins on a fret - rather than stretched on a rack to be dissected.

You really just wish it would end.

But if wishes were always granted, the boy would not have run away to sea, and words like this would not have to be written.

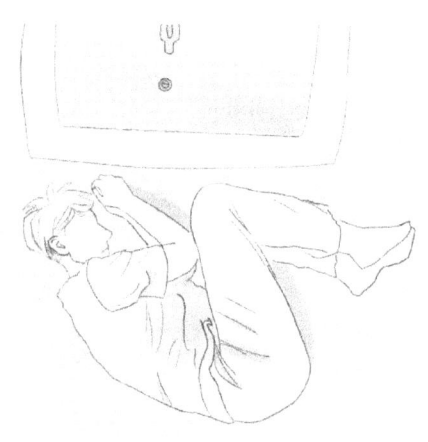

VII

When the boy woke up wrapped around the sink pedestal and floating in tears, he had a terror: it seemed to him that the fears after were worse than the fears during. He thought he might try to outrun the fears, since out-drinking them hadn't worked.

So, he ran. And ran, and ran - and he ran.

He went to somewhere in the middle of Africa by plane alone, and for three weeks he ran on the earth's surface until he made it to the coast, which fortunately was downhill. In that time, the boy had been robbed, been in crashes, seen a man hung, had a man's hand on his rump while he slept, heard a woman give birth on a dhow, and had border guards chasing him to inject him with a deadly needle. He went home to university sunburned, thin, exhausted, yet proud at having survived.

Then he drove across the western continent in two days, taking hitchhikers so he could yell at them and stay awake. He and others in the family drove across Australia one way. Then, when they made the coast, they turned back, and by train and camper drove all the way to another ocean.

He hitchhiked on cars, boats, and potato chip trucks, and accepted rides from troopers and from folks who would have been arrested by troopers except they knew how to blend in. He hitchhiked on the back of pickup trucks so cold he thought his ears might snap off. He sat in the backs of cars filled with Raggedy Ann dolls, and was told to open the glove compartment so many times that it was no longer suspenseful to find guns, magazines, dildoes, handcuffs….

But running away didn't outpace the fear.
The boy was still afraid.

VIII

The boy had another idea. The people who showed him bad things in glove compartments and behind zippers didn't overpower him. In fact, the boy could have out-matched them physically. No, rather, these people had outsmarted the boy.

So, he resolved to outsmart them by reading, thinking, discussing, listening, learning, watching films, learning languages, and experiencing. He learned to give up seats to get free ones later, to walk on board intercity shuttle planes by paying cash and carrying just a sack of gin and tonics for luggage. He learned to save travel credits and to get air miles from his family; it was safer than hitchhiking.

The bright side of his resolve was that he grew smarter and spent time with smart, interesting, experienced people. But the dark side to this, the Yin to the Yang, was that the boy blamed his body for betraying him. He blamed his face and hair for attracting bad people to him. So, he decided that making his mind his strongest muscle wasn't enough—that would enable him to outsmart predators. But if he could be unattractive, not blonde, not faced "so," then they might not approach him to begin with.

So, the boy shaved off his hair. He put a number of cigarettes, filtered and unfiltered, out on his body from his cheek to his ankles, shoulders, many places in between.

He smoked packs a day, and drank most days of the week. He drunkenly set fire to his dorm bed, his backpack, his books, his hands. He tapped cigarette ashes into soda cans while writing, and then drank from the cans.

He drove to the country's capital and back without stopping, except once to pick up a hitcher, and later to have his drugs confiscated and get arrested in a snow-covered parking lot near a highway overpass.

But none of this—the vomiting, the dizziness, the hallucinogenic drugs, the lack of sleep, helped him.

Teachers still came after him. Men still went after him, sometimes because of the brains he was developing.

Nothing seemed to work; his eating became erratic and almost stopped during writing sessions. Blurs came to his vision, about which he gazed at the sky and muttered to himself in public. He went to emergency rooms for help. The boy saw psychiatrists, cut himself alone and in front of people, and pierced his ear with a diaper pin.

Then, while trying to finish his writing assignments before school ended, the boy hardly slept for fourteen days, and lived on just scraps of food, ice cream, coffee, and cigarettes. When he finally finished, he collapsed so deeply for so long that people had to revive him days later.

Just when a therapist would be close to a breakthrough, or a relationship or friendship started to take hold, school would end and he would have to find someone's basement where he could stuff all his books and belongings to free himself up to travel light, using a backpack, a day pack, even a mail sack he found on the highway.

Then one summer day after a decade in various schools, it ended. Without anywhere to keep his books and belongings, he left his library in a dorm lobby, put suitcases and papers on the curb outside a halfway house where they were pried open and scattered down the main avenues for months, had his bicycle stolen, and packed one bookshelf and one case and went home with them. It was over.

For the next year the boy lived afloat; he sailed to an island, to the Arctic coast, on small boats and big boats, to more islands, then home, via a big canal, and across the biggest ocean to the biggest continent. He only slept on land a few weeks in a few places that year—his homes were a dozen sailboats.

IX

    The escapist behavior wasn't enough to change things; the claws squeezing words from him were in too far for him to stop. One place he could run, drink, smoke, and be with smart people who were also running away was aboard sailboats crossing oceans. So, he did that for a few years, meeting many women, but not staying with any of them.

    Every half-decade, he would meet someone so special that he would write about them and to them, but not see them for nearly a year. He was in love with the idea of them, but not them, because he didn't know them.

He hardly knew himself. He was afraid that if he slowed down, they could catch him too, like the men.

So, he didn't slow down.

A life at sea seemed to be the most comfortable. There were three stages to crewing on boats. Knowing nothing was the first, which entailed being in awe, yet also taken advantage of as unpaid crew who could be overworked and underfed. Then there was the middle phase where he knew enough to get paid, manage his own work, and then manage others.

There was nearly a decade in the middle stage in which he built up experience for no tangible reward except room and board. His passports from countries on both sides of the sea began to bulge with extra pages and immigration stamps that looked like official seals or floral patterns.

Finally, if he could demonstrate that he knew a lot about people and things and the sea, and show calm in crises, he could lead a boat as captain and decide the outcomes for himself and all of the others as well. Before his mid-twenties, he attained the highest level, from which one never returns.

His first voyage as captain was across the biggest ocean, took half a year, and convinced the boy that he was better at captaining than he really was. After it, he signed up for three years working with the big tanker ships in Asia. He only went home once a year to sail to the islands again, and during his third trip the boy met a girl in his university town, five years after the only other time they meet. She was so cherubic, so sweet, so lovely, and so pale, with red lips and smiles and an inner pain like his, that he fell in love. He vowed to leave the east for her and returned anyway, even after she demurred. It was another half-decade before they saw one another again for the final time.

Then came 'writing:' the type where one drinks a lot, and talks a lot, and moves a lot, but doesn't actually write a lot. It's hard to pay rent with writing when you don't finish anything, so the boy had to go back to sea in order to get by.

And that was when his rush to embrace death finally produced. He had been running against walls in Africa, Australia, Borneo, India, South and Central America, and in bars and boats from Barbuda to the Roaring Forties and up to the Arctic. Except for minor scrapes and shallow scars, he was pretty unscathed.

Then came hurricanes, and then boats he had no clue how to fix at sea, and crew he'd never met, and owners and brokers he'd either never met, nor ever cared to meet.

And then came mistakes. Injuries—the tip of a finger shorn off from pure stupidity. Danger—so overwhelming that the boy was kneeling in the bottom of the boat and lost control of all the valves in his stressed body.

Then came the boat that burned and then sank, leaving him and the crew swimming away, old and young alike, in terror. And finally, that infuriating bang-snap sound the boat made as if just to enrage the skipper, like an animal demanding attention on a cold November day.

The boy was tired, angry, irritable, scared. He leapt out of his cabin, lunging towards shattered and broken equipment, which was careening wildly off the deck as a snowstorm raged and evening set in. Hubris struck again, as he felt he could control a large out-of-control vessel with his bare hands. He couldn't. Gravity won.

The gear took him over the side. He was flung into the ocean. For the longest time he shivered in his skivvies until he finally found a life ring to cling to. The other boys on board tried to fix the broken boat and save their captain.

The wind streaked the gray northern waves for a long time. No one could get to the boy in time from shore. The boys in the sailboat were losing the fight to get back upwind to him against all that broken mess, and the threat of lines in the propeller which might rip the guts of the boat out and leave them all in the water. Night came on. Fierce winds undulating over the seas were the only sound.

He said to himself—'If you show me safety, if you show me a bed, a piece of land to step foot upon rather than dying here lonely, cold, sad, and scared, I will never worry for the small things again. I will be happy.'

There was nothing except the man-made life ring and the woman-made body of the boy, getting bluer and shakier and number every second. They say that drowning, like birthing, can be very peaceful—just breathe the fluid in. And as he started to drift away, the boy felt his arms being held out, and a force like a saucer pushed up underneath him.

The turtles had heard his whimpers. They came to be sure he didn't drown in tears again.

The turtles knew a place for him.

X

    Many writers would set this scene with the boy lying on a sunny beach, wrapped in kelp, speckled in sand, cradled in the lap or bosom of a mermaid. They would describe survival and domestic details which either they had no experience of, as implausible, as a picket fence on a deserted island, or a note asking for help which doesn't give details of distress, but rather thanks king and country, or faith.

    Instead, this is what you need to know about the island:

The turtles, with some help from the porpoises, nudged, floated, and carried the boy to a smallish island somewhere, like his home, between the eastern continent and the western one.

It was far enough away from any other islands that it was safe from other people, islands, and even hurricanes, cold, and currents.

His island was a stable island, with just enough water, vegetation, and fauna as in meat and fish to catch, kill, cook, and eat. There was only just enough effort required of him and he had what he needed, so long as he didn't injure or harm himself. Waste was re-used whether food uneaten, or eaten and processed, or seaweed or fish offal, encouraging the sandy soil to produce more vitamins for him so that the boy would have teeth to eat, and energy to collect water, and so forth. This was a comfortable but cautious closed circuit of getting by and getting through and getting it done.

We shall call the island 'Smug;' it was almost as though he could have set a watch on a fob by the regularity of its rhythms. It was that time in the middle years of a man's life where his primary duty was duty, and that duty included regularity, reliability, punctuality, and trustworthiness.

Knowing his basic needs were identified and achievable freed up the lad's imagination to consider the world beyond his own. He knew his horizon—what his mind needed was to be able to see beyond it, as he had as a teen, focused on exercising his mind rather than his brawn.

XI

While the boy did not actively miss people, he was curious about what the outside world offered, and what rituals they participated in. Though he was alone the entire time, he was able to enjoy contact with a wider world through what washed up on the shores of the island. He did not alter his rhythms to meet such items. They showed up without warning, and they came at odd intervals.

The first item to wash up on the little island was a basinet, or baby basket. Having not lived with a woman or been parent to a child, and not having any children on the island, the boy was a bit perplexed as to what to do. It seemed like the reed basket floating in the Nile in which a babe was laid in swaddling clothes, or the shoe boxes left in front of fire stations with infants born to adolescents. He decided to use the basinet to store shucked coconuts. They were kept near a spike driven into the ground, so that he could split the husks of the nuts using the spear facing upwards.

Balloons periodically drifted in ocean currents to the isle, but the first one still had air inside it and was struggling over the surface with its thin leash dragging in the waves, barely able to maintain altitude, as in the Wright brothers' experimental craft buffering over sand dunes, or albatrosses using the updraft from ocean swells to stay aloft.

Air in balloons being so different from the air around him, the boy carefully untied the half-filled balloon and inhaled it. But this only transported him to dark places of yore and bad behaviors of the past. And to make it worse, these balloons seemed like jellyfish to his saviors, the sea turtles, so he fastidiously collected any he found and kept them from the ocean. While the balloons may have provided a hit, the boy had outgrown them.

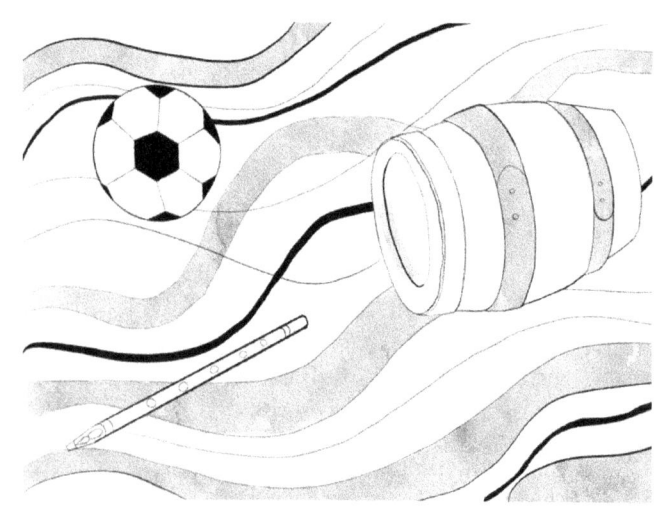

XII

In the middle of the ocean between two continents many things aggregate—the things that float away from land were flotsam, and the things which were thrown or kicked into the sea were called jetsam. One such item was a football, or soccer ball. Depending not on the appearance of the ball, but simply which side of the ocean one is from, determines what you call this item. Though he enjoyed bouncing it from knee to knee and foot to shoulder, the football reminded the boy that he didn't have anyone to play with, and he used it less and less frequently.

Then an ancient-looking wooden item with metal hoops around it bobbed until it was close enough to shore that the boy could retrieve it. It was a large oak cask which smelled of port, sherry, and Madeira wine. Empty on arrival, it was very handy for holding water, his most important survival supply, and for that he used it. The wine smell, however, never fully left the wood.

One day, a flute floated up. This was a wonderful surprise and a source of great joy to the boy, though the reeds were disfigured by the heat and salt water. Still, the music he and his breath and fingers created cheered him greatly. This did not cause him to miss other people, but rather to appreciate his own ability to replace silence with simple melodies.

When he felt the whimsy, the boy would place objects like leaf stems into the holes to alter the timbre, or even a whole leaf to hear what sound the quavering leaf under his breath would make. And he needn't be bothered with a teacher's interference. On his island, the boy was maestro: conductor and audience, composer and critic.

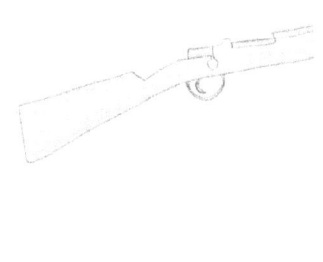

XIII

    A distant storm sent the swells higher as they broke and warped around the island, and it left behind a slim wooden stock of a traditional bolt-action carbine rifle, from those days of colonial wars. Was it from the Veld, or Mafcking in South Africa, or perhaps the Black Hole of Calcutta, or a Napoleonic war, or a lonely sentry outpost on a stone frigate like Ascension or Bermuda? Or an airfield in Cape Juby or a redoubt at Khartoum, a windblown tent beside Scott in Antarctica, or the Rock of Ariamazes which Alexander the Great overwhelmed with alpinists to claim Roxanne as his bride like Rapunzel?

In any event, with no one or nothing to kill, no one to contest his ownership or fight over companionship as on Pitcairn Island, the boy had no need for a rifle. He used the butt of the gun stock to grind down seeds like a pestle and tenderize the bivalves and conch he harvested from the sea, and break the shells of crawfish tails. In any event, where was he to have found the metal to melt into bullets? And what, or who, was he to shoot at? If there was a civil war on the island, he would lose twice.

An old book washed up with thick panels which kept it afloat. It had been written in ink, and the seas of the north and south had washed the words clear. This gave the boy a tabula rasa to start fresh; to write his own story.

XIV

A plastic flower in a cheap bouquet with vibrant and almost-convincing tropical colors drifted up. Yet, the boy already had genuine floral blooms on his island, and though some had small thorns, who could begrudge them? He pushed the flowers off into the ocean, with no need of them and only the wish that they might bring to another a smile on perhaps an island without flowers, or a mantel upon which they might rest, or a vase into which they could be placed.

There came, one day, a pair of lingerie; it made the boy think of bank robbers who pulled them over their heads to hide their identity. He did find a purpose for it—to sieve out the seeds from citrus fruit and extract the most from those precious fruits. Also, he could hang the lingerie legging between branches and place fruit into them so they would not bruise, and could remain aired and less likely to rot and attract flies—he turned it into a hammock.

The currents have their own songs and rhythms and are the great livers and kidneys of the planet; in such a way, the oceans place similarly-sized items and materials in the same currents. This creates beaches filled with bottle caps or bays of unmatched sandals, or coves clogged with seaweed. And so it was that soon after the plastic flowers, there arrived a light plastic ornament showing a man in tuxedo with dark skin embracing a similarly-toned woman in a long white dress.

It was a decoration from atop a wedding cake, perhaps fallen from a passenger ship, washed from a beach house, or carried by hand into the ocean for a phosphorescent skinny-dip by the newlyweds and released into the seas like a turtle hatchling. The boy kept the figurine, placing it atop a flat shelf near where he slept in such a way that for a week each month, the moon served as a backdrop to the couple and bathed them in gentle blue-gray light. This made the boy ⟨...⟩istfully but, rather, shyly, as this was a ⟨...⟩ had not plumbed, for which he might, ⟨...⟩eacher.

Many months later an epaulet arrived, showing three gold stripes of a first officer, who must have had it pulled off when disembarking an amphibious aircraft, or might have had to ditch into the ocean. Perhaps the craft splashed down in a space capsule and in the rush to escape once they blew the doors, it fell off her shoulder and into the sea.

To the boy it seemed like an oversized caterpillar; he was king and prince and pauper on this little island and had no need to fantasize about power: to steal it, be elected, or resent or glory in it. Power held no power on the island. The boy used the epaulet to scrub the bowls he had fashioned of the limestone rock and driftwood.

When storms ravage low countries, particularly those along rivers where the living cannot bury their dead deeply, graves are torn asunder and opened. Caskets, particularly the well-sealed ones, wash out of the earth and to the surface. Storms strong enough to wrest the dead from below to atop the surface of the planet are commensurately strong enough to carry the caskets out to sea. The boy knew this from his mariner days, when far from land, passing the mouths of great rivers they would find farm animals on trees, and bloated bodies of all types floating swollen in the sun.

The boy found a casket which bumped asho on the little island. Fortunately, years of being toss the waves had pried the contents out, and onl wood remained. The boy used this durable wood for shelving in his living are and fashioned a smaller box from it which he used as a trunk for those items of driftwood or his own manufacture which he wished to keep, to preserve and perhaps even one day pass on to other boys or girls to visit the island.

XV

There are many languages spoken along the rim of the ocean in which the boy lived; some with roots in Iberian, Celtic, Anglo, Francophone, Scandinavian, Thule, Kalaallisut, Yoruba, Wolof, Creole, Arabic, Icelandic, Akan, ǂKxʼaullʼeln, and more. So, the boy was pleasantly surprised a message his language after several years on the island. A translucent bulbous-bottomed ginger beer bottle from yesteryear bobbed ashore at his feet. It was firmly corked, and within it was a yellow parchment, dry and crisp.

The boy popped out the cork and managed, by using the antennae of a crawfish, to pincher and nudge the paper out of the bottle's neck and into his hands. Excitedly, he read its message:

One must not only find and take;

but also give, share, and grow.

We don't only need to be at the summit to reach the sun,

we also need the shade of other trees,

and deep roots to stay grounded and not be swept away.

Each of us has a gift: your gift is to write;

to share by writing.

You mustn't drown your gift in gin,

or let your gift float in tears,

nor let the storms tear your gift from the earth and send it to sea.

You must harness your gift as a wind to sails,

steer it to other boys and girls,

it is yours to share, so share it.

A gift is more than something to take;
taking is for children,
giving is for the gifted.

XVI

That night the boy lay on his back under the stars, looking up in wonder. He looked past the wedding cake couple to the moon. He wondered how many other children were watching that same moon at that same moment.

From the sheltered water nearby, the boy heard a short sound which started abruptly, as though it were being forced through a sluice, and then it ended with a sigh, like water from a dam. He knew the sound—it was the sharp inhale followed by the luxuriant exhale of adult turtles—the large kind that grazed on the grass of the bay.

As she had often done before, a large turtle flapped and flopped her way to the same beach that she had been hatched from decades earlier. As an albatross does not see land for six years, only she sea turtles leave the sea to nest; the males never leave the sea. And the boy knew it wasn't the season for turtles to lay eggs.

He took the book drained of words, filled only with empty pages. He wrapped it tightly in sail cloth, and slung it over his shoulder. He walked from his stockade towards the turtle, which was already making its way to the nearby sea, down a gentle slope of white sand rendered pinkish by broken coral.

When the turtle entered the shallow bay, the boy followed. Then, as his eyes adjusted, he saw that there were several large turtles in the bay; a bale of them; a flotilla. Beyond them was a pod of porpoises who would act like destroyers or frigates, and further out assembled a glide of flying fish to act as an outer screen for the voyage ahead. Above patrolled a colony, or scavenging of seagulls, the speckled grays being adolescent and thus covering the rear.

The boy lay in the warm water and gently placed his hands on either side of the mama turtle's scute, like the collar behind her neck.

The turtles were taking him home, and to other people; for what is writing without sharing it with someone to read it?

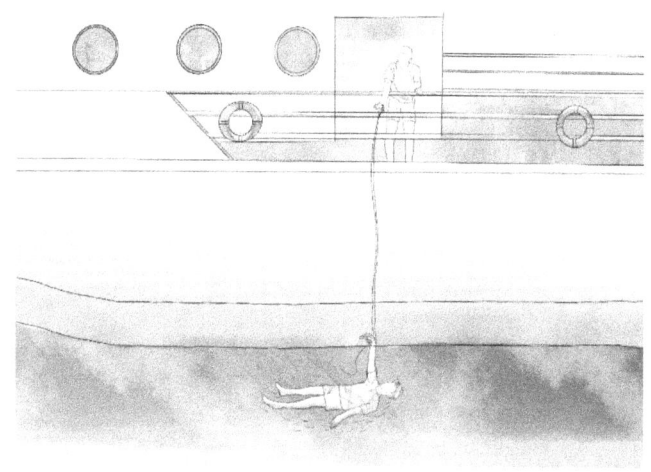

XVII

The last gray tendrils of the twilight were being pulled across the broad eastern horizon when the boys in the sailboat spotted their captain.

He was motionless, sprawled across a life ring, with snow and gulls swirling over him. As they grasped him by the arms and hair and pulled him up from the float, they were startled to hear a loud exhale.

The turtles hovered beneath him as the porpoises and the rest of the cavalcade bid the boy their goodbye. During his voyage back to the sailboat, they protected the boy as one of their own. Like the protectors, and unlike the predators who should have protected him in youth, the sea life and island life had cleansed him of his worries and fears. They allowed him time to answer the riddles he struggled with in a safe place.

    Now the boy had no need for them, because he had, in fact, been able to swim like a turtle—to go to them half-dead and return fully alive. His inner strength had been there all along—he just hadn't heard its call until now. He knew that the life he had always wanted to live had been his to behold all along. And he embraced it standing up, not on bended knee.

XVIII

The boy wrote this book to share, for you to read. One day you may write a book of your own, to tell us what you were given, and what you make of it all. Or you may share your gift in other ways. Whatever we choose to do with our gift, whether we diminish or develop it, it is ours. It is yours.

Your gift is as truly yours as you are you. It is what we leave when the casket is empty. It is what we make of the wood. It is the dream we see behind the stars of the figurines, and the music we make. It is the gun we shoulder, or the pestle we grind, and the balloons we blow, and what the balloons blow out of us. It makes the sound of our inhale and also of our exhale.

protectors, and unlike the predators who should have protected him in youth, the sea life and island life had cleansed him of his worries and fears. They allowed him time to answer the riddles he struggled with in a safe place.

Now the boy had no need for them, because he had, in fact, been able to swim like a turtle—to go to them half-dead and return fully alive. His inner strength had been there all along—he just hadn't heard its call until now. He knew that the life he had always wanted to live had been his to behold all along. And he embraced it standing up, not on bended knee.

XVIII

The boy wrote this book to share, for you to read. One day you may write a book of your own, to tell us what you were given, and what you make of it all. Or you may share your gift in other ways. Whatever we choose to do with our gift, whether we diminish or develop it, it is ours. It is yours.

Your gift is as truly yours as you are you. It is what we leave when the casket is empty. It is what we make of the wood. It is the dream we see behind the stars of the figurines, and the music we make. It is the gun we shoulder, or the pestle we grind, and the balloons we blow, and what the balloons blow out of us. It makes the sound of our inhale and also of our exhale.

For some, a basinet will be filled with little heartbeats, and for others fruit in husks. Some will master the flick of a sports ball, while others are unable to make it onto the field. The cask can keep us afloat on the barren surface of the sea, or it can drown us, if we let it. Lingerie can be for squeezing into, or for squeezing fruit out of.

Plastic flowers to a florist may seem off color, but to the Bantu and San people of the Kalahari Desert, they might be a marvel during the dry. Even a blank book held upside down might invite someone to inquire about its contents if you read it alone in a convivial place.

Books can anchor, yes: but they can also fly.

Epaulets telegraph a hierarchy, but each of us guides our path through the reefs and across the waves. With the help of turtles, dolphins, and birds, perhaps we find our way to shore much of the time. There are times for us to bend to our knees, as with sharing our gift. When and how we choose to bow is ours—and only ours—to decide.

www.ingramcontent.com/pod-product-compliance
Lightning Source LLC
Chambersburg PA
CBHW072137070526
44585CB00016B/1721